BOOK BENCHERS
PUBLICATIONS
PRESENTS

LOVE

LOVING

LOVED

AYUSH MONDAL

AELAY PUBLICATION

A dream come true for every writers out there. We spot every possible problem for the writers, help in rectifying them and guide them towards the best outcome. We make sure to understand your needs, dreams and expectations, and nourish them with our services and stop not until we fulfill your dreams. The writers have a right and freedom to choose what they want here. They have us to guide them through the hardest path untill the end. Believe in us.

Aelay Publication - by a writer for the writers.

BOOK BENCHERS

Book Benchers is the affiliate of Aelay publication. Both the publication is handled by Astro.
Aelay plays the role of publishing solo books.
And Book Benchers is epically for publishing anthologies.

Book Benchers have 2 different teams.

1. Tamil
2. English/Hindi

Never mind what our main motive is to help all the budding writers, who are seeking for their dream of publishing their own book to come true.

We are there to help out everyone.
In guiding for starting up with your carrier in compiling until finishing up your full book.

COPYRIGHT

(Affiliate by Aelay Publish)

Book: LOVE LOVING LOVED
Compiler: AYUSH MONDAL
First Edition: Augest 2021

Published By:

The Book Benchers
5/175, Fathima nagar,
Kuthenkuly,
Tirunelveli -627104
Phone: 9944992571

Design And Executed by

ISBN : 978-93-5533-090-1
Page : 135

<u>Acknowledgement</u>

Acknowledgement is essential to boost up passion, making person more valid and precious, giving the team a great progress that makes worth.

We would like to use this opportunity to thank each and everyone who all the people involved in this book and, more specifically, to all the co - authors .Without your support, this book would not have become a reality.

We would like to thank each one of the authors for their contributions. Our sincere gratitude to all who contributed their time and expertise to this book.

We wish to acknowledge the valuable contributions of the Publication regarding the improvement of quality, coherence, and content. Last but not least, we would like to extend our gratitude to parents and friends who have been a huge support through the book.

<u>FOUNDER</u>

IRUDAGA ASTRO

Irudaga Astro, From Tirunelveli, Founder of
Aelay and BB (Book Benchers)
He had completed his BE.
He has written 3 Tamil poetry book's which
hits the top list on social media!
His main aim is to allow the writers to
publish their words as their book rather than
just Posting them on Insta.

LINK AND POSTER MAKER

CATHERINE ASMI T

Catherine Asmi T, From Tirunelveli
She has completed her M.com
Her passion is Drawing and Designing.

Book Benchers

TEAM HEAD

She is a passionate writer from Chennai. Writing makes her pressure go away. She had played the role of co-author for more than 100+ Antho's. She would like to thank her parents and her Loveable Brother for supporting her rather than stopping her from what she wanted to do! For being the main reason for achieving her dreams. As well as for standing beside her in all the ups and downs. Whenever she feels like she needs to get out of her stressful timing or feels like she needs peacefulness, she starts to paint, she would never mind sitting in the same place for so many hours when it comes to her painting. She believes that anyone could hurt her, But never her books could!!

Catch her in Insta and FB
Insta: @theinnocentheart
FB: KA. PARINASRI

<u>Index</u>

Compiler's Name:

AYUSH MONDAL

Co-author's List

1. Sanjay Naik
2. Lipsa Dabhi
3. Dolly Vadhvani
4. Dipa Sharma
5. Athira. A
6. Amritanshu Shreshth
7. Har Deepansh Bahadur Sinha
8. Shaswat Sourav Sahoo
9. Sonal Prajapati
10. Kushagra Pathak
11. Dakeekun Funmilayo
12. Harshita Verma
13. U.Muthupriya
14. Rajkumar.G
15. Poetry Khakholia
16. Ankita Mishra
17. Ankita Vibhor Garg

18. Ankur Mishra
19. Sravani Kommayya
20. Prachi Gupta
21. Ankita Nahar
22. Naveen Bhardwaj
23. Sohini Ghosh
24. Anjaan Kumar Dinkar
25. U.Abishek
26. Ankita Sarkar
27. YuvaSri Yelleti
28. Rozy Paul
29. Manisha Kamaraj
30. Sakina Husain Asghar
31. Shweta Singh
32. Samyuktha S.
33. Nikita Yadav
34. Dr.Shweta Singh
35. S.Nandhinee
36. Kajal Bhargav
37. Ravishanker Nishad (ARVI)
38. Meenakshi
39. Deesha Soni
40. Yogesh Gurjar Chinu
41. Shivang Sharma
42. Bhargavi. V
43. Catherine Sheena
44. Srija Sadhukhan
45. Nikhil Jain
46. Soniya Varghese
47. Akkshaya Prasanna
48. Akshaya Murugesan

49. Payal Kamdi
50. Anamika
51. Vaishnawi Kumari
52. Pragati giri
53. Dr. Seema Dansana
54. Jasmine Panda

AYUSH MONDAL

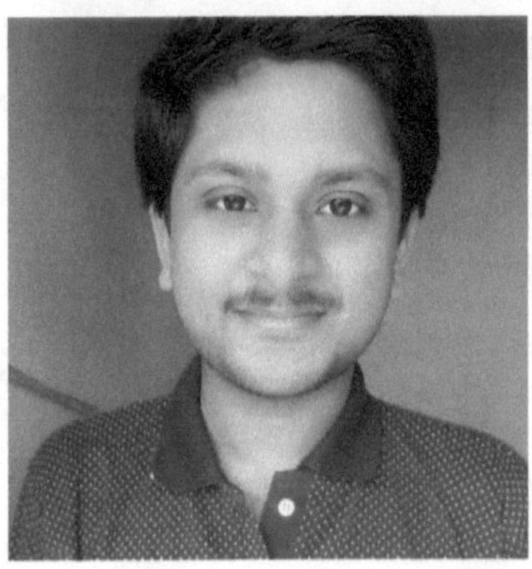

AYUSH MONDAL, He is studying in B.Com Honors from BRSNC Collage, Barrackpore. He lives in Kolkata, West Bengal (North 24 pgs). He gain more experience through the journey of writing and he wants to learn more. He writes many Poems and Quotes and Short Stories and he is still writing to improve his skills more. Currently, he is working in many different Anthologies about different topics and he is grateful to be a part of this Anthology. He participated in many anthologies as a co-author and he has written many Poems and Stories. Now he is working as a compiler but still he is focusing in his writing. He has a passion to write everything. He always says, "Age is just a number, it can never judge you what you can write." He writes all his poems in both Hindi and English language that his poems touch the heart of the readers.

Follow him on: Instagram - ayuman2002
Facebook - Ayush Mondal

PLACE OF THE HEART

I have a beautiful heart inside of body
Full of love and happiness and joy
Can't be found, a single sign of sorrow
Here, exists only your appearance
Where, you get the place in my heart
You will live there always, for a long time
And you will stay with me for the life time
So far away from the vast world
Far away, from the selfish people
Where, true love doesn't exist anymore
As, the people don't have the human heart
Where the pure love actually exists
The people can never understand that
But you will be happy always, in my heart
With lots of feelings and true emotions
There's a big photo frame of yours
On the walls of my heart, you can see
Free from all unwanted things of the world
No need, no need of unnecessary things
Where, you can live in peace forever.

1. SANJAY NAIK

Sanjay Naik is from Kharagpur State of West Bengal. He is an Economics graduate (Hons), a writer from the heart and passionate about singing. Through the platform of anthology, he wants to spread love & positivity among his readers and wants to heal his readers' hearts with his magical words. Sanjay is at utmost peace when he pens his emotions. He believes that the power of his words will heal the wounds of many readers. Till now participated in 200+ Anthologies as a CO-AUTHOR. He is Compiler of anthology "SELF HAPPINESS" , "SCREAM" & " SARANG". And now compiled more than 50 + Anthologies. Instagram:- @the_poetry_wo

I WISH YOU WERE MINE!!

Where do everyone's
Wishes come true?
Some spread their hands
In front of God and some
Accept it from the heart,
If someone's heart is broken,
Then somewhere it connects,
Is that the heart you've longed for?
Does he have the power to?
Understand your feelings?

Such a sea where you have
To drown and also save yourself
Love is a beautiful gift which
Is not in everyone's share,
The person who got they are lucky
To be immersed in his thoughts,
To smile thinking of him,
This is the identity of your
Heart's satisfaction.

Love has to be kept in
Someone's memories,
Love is to become the
Happiness of someone's face,
Let's go together on such a
Journey where I can cry
Peacefully by keeping my
Head on your shoulder.

2. LIPSA DABHI

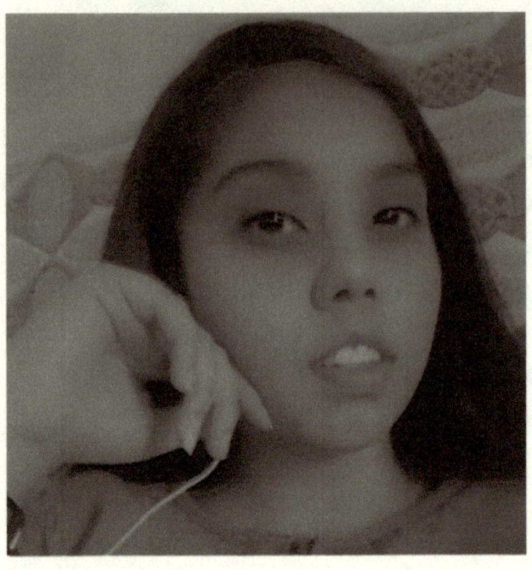

She is Lipsa Dabhi. She is Author and also good Co-Author. She is eighteen years old; she is student of the computer engineering. She is extraordinary person. She is always good leader. Her mam mrunal prajapati is her inspiration person and also her motivater, her friend Chetna raval also supported to her and her mom Manisha Ben and her father Nilesh Bhai also supported to her for any type of her creativity. She also wrote poems, short stories, shayaries. Her writing skills almost very well and her creative collections are always best.

LIFE WITH LOVE

Life with love is extraordinary,
Life is wonderful and beauty,
Life with love is extra beautiful,
Life with love is good forever.

Love is precious in life,
So every moment enjoy with love and happiness,
Life is good with truth love,
So stay with love.

Life with love is extra perfect,
Perfect life with perfect person and forever time,
Every moment on life enjoy with love,
Life is great stay with happiness, joy, fun and love.

एक तरफा छिपा हुआ प्यार

आज तक प्यार को मेरे एक तरफा रखा हैं मैं ने,
ना नाम दिया उसे कोई,
छिपा हुआ सा रखा प्यार मेरा,
इसीलिए कभी वो दो तरफा बना ही नहीं ।

प्यार को मेरे एक तरफा सा रहना पड़ा,
एक बार इजहार किया था उससे प्यार का वो तो मझाक
समझकर बैठा,
इस कदर प्यार एक तरफा रह गया ।

छूपा ना पाए तुझे कही ऐसा राझ हो तुम,
मेरे दिल में बसनेवाला पहला प्यार हो तुम,
हर कोई फिका लगता मुझे तेरे आगे,
ऐसे ही रह गया छिपा प्यार मेरा ।

3. DOLLY VADHVANI

नमस्कार, इनका नाम डोली वाधवाणी है ! ये आंनद गुजरात से हैं ! इन्होंने गुजरात युनिवर्सिटी गांधीनगर से B.Com और सोमनाथ युनिवर्सिटी से PGDCA किया है ! अभी दो साल से Computer Operator की तरह जोब कर रहीं हैं ! डोली को अपनी भावनाएं लिखना बेहद पसंद है !

इनकी जिंदगी का एक ही असूल है,

तुम आज को जियो और आज मे जियो फिर देखो जिंदगी कितनी खूबसूरत है...!

प्यार है तुमसे...।

सुनो ना प्यार है तुमसे ।
पूरा नही पर बेइंतहा है तुमसे ।

झुकी सी नजरों से तूझे देखना ।
तेरे लिए नजरें झूका लेना ।
यही हाल है कब से ।

तूझसे मिलने के लिए तडपना ।
तेरे पास आते ही दिल का धडकना ।
ये कमाल है कब से ।

तेरे मुस्कुराते ही मेरा हर गम भूल सा जाना ।
तूझे उदास देखते ही मेरा मुरझा सा जाना ।

तेरे साथ चलने का ख़्वाब सा देखना ।
हर वक्त तूझे महसूस सा करना ।

रात के अंधेरो मे या दिन के उजालों मे ।
तेरे साये का साथ सा होना ।
ये भी पसंद है हमें ।

तेरे हर ख़्वाब और ख्यालो से प्यार है हमें ।
तेरा ही इंतजार है हमें ।

तूझसे प्यार है हमें ।
पूरा नही बेइंतहा है हमें ।

4. DIPA SHARMA

She is a teacher by profession and currently running her own tutorial named as "Sanwariya Tutorials". She is very positive and fun loving person. Her first quote book is "तेरी शरण" which is dedicated to Khatu ShyamJi. Her first solo poetry book "Broken (No rebuilding myself) is going to be published soon. She has successfully completed two anthologies named "Phoenix (Reborn from your ashes)" and "Your Therapeutic Love" .She has been part of many anthologies. In this book she tried to pen down her thoughts, hope you all like it. You can read her thoughts on Instagram @radhika47605

I paint my scars with glitters
To make them more shiny,
More attractive and more beautiful
Because, I love them
They give me the strength to
Fight and remind me that I survived.
They remind me of the time
When people tried to break me
But they failed.......
My scar made me complete

****

Dear heart,
I know you are fragil
Still you are the strongest
Muscle in by body
Every time you break
You made me stronger
You shatter over and over still you live
Because there is nothing stronger than you
We will survive both you and me...

5. ATHIRA. A

Co-author Athira, A is a young poetess from Ernakulam, Kerala State. She has completed her Bachelors in Science stream from St. Teresa's College, Ernakulam. She has been writing poems for 15 years as her passion. Book reading and reviewing is also her major hobby.

Email: - athiraorminnu@gmail.com

HER LOVE

She loved me the most,
Even more than herself.
But what did I do to her?
I dodged her the most.

She laughed her heart out,
Even when she was in pain.
But what did I give her?
I wounded her the most.

She cherished me a lot,
As if I was her divine being,
With all her love in the eyes
And all her care in the heart.

But I was the only one
Who never ever perceived
The ardour she had for me,
The disquiet she felt for me.

NOTES OF LOVE

My beloved, do you know,
How many notes of love
That I have written for you
Are left with me unsent?

There are these days,
When thoughts of you
Keep rushing within me,
Like uproaring waves.

The memories of days
We had spent together,
Arise in me the impulse
To meet you once again.

Alas! It will never happen;
It wasn't you, who had left,
But the hapless fate had
Stolen you away from me.

6. AMRITANSHU SHRESHTH

Master Amritanshu Shreshth is a student of Open Minds A Birla School Kankarbagh, Patna, Bihar std. 10 with an excellent academic performance and a distinguished skill in sports. With a magnificent start at the age of 12 he is an avid writer with a keen interest in life lessons and classical literature with some specific hobbies like playing guitar. He loves to express his feelings and life lessons with his write-ups. He had won many medal and certificates in Literature and Debates with his writing and speaking skills and had written many articles and science documentaries with his pen name Yuvraj.

YOUR DECISION MATTERS

If you think you should suicide,
Note a point that many people threw aside,
They regret it even now gasping for a last try,
Even after knowing that they lost their try they cry
with open eye,
Looking in the sky thinking how they eagerly flew,
By gathering some courage they could have passed
through.

If you think you should suicide,
Note a point that many people threw aside,
Driven by the hell for making other people regret,
Your choice matter to all whom you forget,
They live for you not for themselves,
They make the real world appear to you by using
their spells.

If you think you should suicide,
Note a point that many people threw aside,
No-one would stop you for doing so,
But you won't be able to die again wherever you go,
You will always be ashamed for what you did,
You could have lived strong and make problems no
more than a kid.

MY INCOMPLETE STORY

I left my story incomplete,
Waiting for someone whom I can greet.
In the lanes of loneliness and darkness,
Lost in the shadows of discrete,
I found a source of light to harness.

It was none other than my mother,
Who not only helped me to stand on my feet,
But also to outrage and compete.
Finally looked the sky with nothing to bother.

Then came the last evening
The one from which I can never recover,
That was the day when the world was screening,
And believed something that can never be
uncovered.

Still remember that last evening which I
encountered,
When my mother went in dark light,
After teaching me how to fight,
I was out in the world living without her,
But she was still there in the quiet night whether
wrong or right.

7. HAR DEEPANSH BAHADUR SINHA

He is Har Deepansh Bahadur Sinha. He belongs to Lucknow, UP. He is a research scholar of Oceanography and has done masters in Geography from National Post Graduate College. Completed his schooling from Study Hall. His hobbies are art , listening to music , cooking & loads of driving.His interest areas are Astronomy, Writing, Photography & Travelling a lot.

SELF LOVE

Loving yourself is literally necessary
We think it's too ordinary,
We don't keep our care
I think this is not fair.

We must give ourselves some time
For that we don't need to quarantine,
Always do forgive yourself
Let's be happy with ourself.

Treat your body like a princess
Nothing is wrong in being obsessed,
Keep your spirit fearless
Celebrations should be endless.

Bring yourself to yourself a bit closer
Definitely you will get a blooming exposure,
It's our journey and our own life
Be the first preference and first choice.

Don't hesitate in what others will say
Just keep pampering oneself and slay.

MY FIRST PROPOSAL

I was enjoying my college life
Came in contact with my future wife,
It was the season of chilled winters
She knocked my heart and wanted to enter.

For the first time I felt for a girl
She was alluring just like a pearl,
Days passed away we came closer
I got extremely phenomenal exposure.

One day she suddenly proposed
For her my love got exposed,
Her eyes were reflecting devotion
And her lips showed emotions.

A brand new journey got started
Literally she is very kind hearted,
Now I was completely caged
Since, we both got engaged.

So finally we tied the knot
Believe me stars has no fault.

8. SHASWAT SOURAV SAHOO

Shaswat Sourav Sahoo, is an eighteen-something adventurer who grew up traversing the wonders through the pages of metaphors. He fell in love with books and never reverted. Today he is pursuing his studies and living a clichéd life at NISER as an Integrated M.Sc. research scholar. He has been recently awarded with the Global Achiever's Award. When he is not surrounded by words you can spot him fancying and pampering the dogs.He is a jovial kind of person revamping his past grief events into allured moments. He loves voicing his emotions and get it penned down. Another feather to his cap is his intense intimacy with taking shots. Nevertheless, he is also impassioned for painting, playing indoors, origami. He is looking forward his life being a polymath and pours on whatever he possesses within and wishes never to quell it.

THE BETRAYAL

I loved her from all my heart
Leaving no place
For others to be a part
Yet she broke my heart

Besieged by grief and sorrows
Rejected me, pain followed
Depressed was me and broken
My definition for love verbally narrowed

I stood up and had my head
Straight and nothing to fear ahead
It's just a lesson that made me fed
Gear up boy, the champ within you
Has been unleashed
Lengthen your stride
And bounce yourself to the peak
Clutching all your pride.

9. SONAL PRAJAPATI

I am Sonal Prajapati living in Delhi. Electrical Engineer by profession and writer by passion. I had been part of online writing contest and more than 50 + Anthology. for my more quotes, poems, shayari, & stories follow me on instagram -misswriter_

MY WORLD

My day starts from you and end on you.
Everyone loves me for my nature
But who I loved is all matter.
Clearing all pain that i have
Dancing with me in the rain
Holding my hands on way
I just closed my eyes & run away
Drinking tea in same cup
Taking our career in up
Fighting for me in the ring
He always pay for what I bring
A behind hug from him
Remind me of everything
You always make me pride
You are the one who never lie
Taking me with you on ride
He always stays on my side

10. KUSHAGRA PATHAK

इनका नाम कुशाग्र पाठक है । ये लखनऊ से हैं । ये तृतीय वर्ष के छात्र हैं । ये 20 वर्ष के थे तब से लेखन का कार्य कर रहे हैं । ये बहुत से लेखको से प्रेरित हैं लेकिन सबसे ज्यादा ये कुमार विश्वास जी से प्रेरित हैं । इनका लिखना शुरू करने का उद्देश्य लोगों कि मदद करना और लोगों को मदद करने के लिए तैयार करना है । ये मुख्य रूप से सामाजिक और विभिन्न लोगों कि मानसिकता के बारे में लिखते हैं ।

माँ का प्यार

तेरे चरणों को छूकर ।।
यू तुझसे लिपट कर ।
इतने वर्षों के बाद भी मैं ,फिर से बच्चा बन जाता हूँ माँ ।।

तेरे आँचल का छाया पा कर ।।
तेरे गोद की फिर से माया पा कर ।
छोर छाड कर सबकुछ मैं ,फिर से अच्छा बन जाता हूँ माँ ।।

गुजर कर सारी ऊपर नीचे की बस्ती से भी ।।
काले सागर मे अपनी ही टूटी कस्ती से भी ।
तेरे लिए दुनिया में हर बार मैं ,सबसे सच्चा बन जाता हूँ माँ ।।

हर किसी के नफरत के बाद भी ।।
खुद मेरी कुछ काली हसरत के बाद भी ।
पाकर तेरी ममता की छाया मैं ,फिर से अच्छा बन जाता हूँ माँ
।।

कैसे देखू तेरे आँशु जो मेरे मोती है ।।
मेरी लिये तू रात भर भी नहीं सोती है ।
लहू की एक बूद पर ही मैं , दुआवों से लिपटा गुच्छा बन जाता
हूँ माँ ।।

मैं रोता हूँ तो तुम तो भी रोती है ।।
मेरे आशुओं से अपना पल्लु भिगोती है ।
मत हो परेशान तू ,तेरे लिए अच्छा मैं बच्चा बन जाता हूँ माँ ।।

11. DAKEEKUN FUNMILAYO

Dakeekun Funmilayo is a young writer who resides in Nigeria, a West Africa country. She loves writing poetry and stories. Her hobby is tourism. She has many poems and stories in her name

REMEMBER ME

As the day pass by
As long as the sun shines
And the moon is bright
You'll remember me
My straight long hair
My skin forever fair
My bright small eyes
And my dress always
Neatly pressed

You'll remember my sweet voice
And recognize it among millions
You'll remember my breath
Underneath your neck
You'll remember my
Forever radiant smile
Ever shining from adorable grace

And for eternity i will
Stick in you like the pleura
Of your heart.

12. HARSHITA VERMA

Co-author Harshita Verma is a writer from Lucknow. She has completed her graduation in commerce stream. She has been writing poetry for the last few years as her passion. She wants to be a novelist in future.

LOVE

The heart beating wildly
The world looking beautiful
The flowers smelling heavenly
Still my love unexpressed but true

The sense of a different feeling
The realization of first love of life
The mind finding answers to this
But not able to express the feelings itself

The happiness of the first love
Unable to express feelings
Still a little hope in the mind
That you will understand

It hurts not able to tell you
The love of mine for you
Still a different feeling and hope of
Forever living in this world of love.

13. U.MUTHUPRIYA

She is U.Muthupriya.she has completed M.A.English.she is working as an Assistant Professor.she has more interest on writing short stories

FRIENDS FOR LIFE

We have been friends together,
In sunshine and shade;
Since first beneath the chestnut-trees,
In infancy we played.
But coldness dwells within my heart'
A cloud is on thy brow;
We have been friends together –
Shall a light word part us now?

We have been gay together;
We have laugh'd at little jests;
For the fount of hope was gushing
Warm and joyous in our breasts.
But laughter now hath fled thy lip,
And sullen groups thy brow;
We have been gay together –
Shall a light word part us now?

We have been sad together,
We have wept, with better tears,
O'er the grass-grown graves, where
Slumber'd
The hopes of early years.
The voices which are silent there
Would bid thee clear thy brow;
We have been sad together-
Oh! What shall part us now?

14. RAJKUMAR.G

G.Raj Kumar is an English Literature Graduate and Assistant Professor of English, has been working with writing challenged clients for over three years. He loves the way how Francis Kafka pens his Letters. He provides verse writing and article writing based on Delight and persuasion. His educational background in English Literature and Humanities has given him a broad base to write on a broad perspective.

TO MY SWEET COUSIN
WHO DESERVES MY LOVE

To my Sweet Cousin who deserve my Love
Sweet cousin, with a delightful grin,
Like you're remarkable and extremely cool style.
You're not just sweet and kind,
Shoes marked down, you can discover.

Valuable cousin, I love you beyond a doubt,
As a companion and genuinely.
I'm so happy, when you're near,
My dearest companion, I have found.

Creature darling, I should say,
With charming little dogs, you love to play.
Helping other people, unselfishly act,
Wonderful highlights consistently pull in.

Playing music, somewhere down in your spirit,
Goal-oriented Man, more than one objective.
Personally, you straightforwardly develop,
About existence, there's such a lot of you know.

Snags for us are rarely excessively little,
Support one another, when we stagger and fall.
At the point when I feel like others were mean,
On your shoulder, I can generally lean.

Bliss and satisfaction you unreservedly bring,
Such a lot of fun, together we sing.
Whatever the future, may bring us or hold,

With you close by, I wouldn't fret going downhill.
I had no words to say
To the words you had
We are cousins
Savoring our transgressions.

You, who needed this to go on
I, who needed this to all end,

You, whom I really focused on so much since I
watched you develop,
I, whom you required wrongly and mistakenly,.

I love you Mr.Kishy

15. Poetry Khakholia

नमस्कार, ये है पोइट्री खाखोलिया गुवाहाटी असम से, बीयालिस वर्ष, कॉन्वेंट एजुकेटेड , शादीशुदा दो बच्चे है। इन्होंने एमकॉम, म.इड, एलएलबी किया है पर लिखना इनकी रुचि रही है स्कूल से ही और अब इसी क्षेत्र में एक मुकाम अर्जित करना चाहती। इन्होंने चालीस से ज्यादा अंथोलॉजी में अपनी लेखनी से नवाजा है और कहानी किताब भी लिख रही है जो जल्द ही आने वाली। लिखना सिर्फ काम नहीं बल्कि जुनून है इनके लिए जो ये हर पल जीती। आशा है आप सभी को इनकी रचना पसंद आए।

कुछ खास फर्क नहीं पड़ता

कुछ खास फर्क नहीं पड़ता
किसी के हाथ छुड़ा के चले जाने से ।
हां वो तो उसको पूछो जिसका हाथ
छुड़ा के गया है उसपे क्या गुजरी
क्या कहर ही मचा वो तो वहीं जाने ।

जाने वाले तो चले जाते वो क्यूं कब
सोचने लगे पीछे क्या खालीपन
वीरानी रह जाती ।
एक लंबा अर्सा अब यूं ही गुजरेगा
जैसे कि इश्क़ मुझे ही था ।
पर अब सोचती हूं
क्यूं था ।

16. ANKITA MISHRA

I am Ankita Mishra from Cuttack, Odisha. I am a student pursuing my graduation in bachelor's of commerce. Writing was never my passion nor my hobby. All I loved was singing, crafting and playing badminton. Then when I used to stay alone I used to write my feelings no matter happy or sad. And that's how I started writing by expressing my thoughts, feelings and emotions into words. I just hope and look forward towards taking this habit as my passion.

A SYMBOL OF LOVE.

Rose is not just a flower,
But a symbol of love.
We will fly together,
Higher than the dove.

Your love has filled,
My life with happiness.
Just like a rose fills,
The room with fragrance.

Though the rose have thorns in it,
Still it blooms so beautiful.
We too came up blooming,
By crossing all the obstacles.

Now the grieving time had passed,
And our love is cast.
Let's built our flower bed,
With bush of roses red.

YOU ARE MY TEDDY

Hey my dear love,
You are my cute teddy.
Just want to hold you tight,
And get cozy.

So many things to say and do,
Wishing I could hold you.
My hearts is only for you,
Feeling like a dream come true.

Happy or sad my heart,
Always needs you.
Angry or in agony my mind,
Never stops thinking about you.

The world is yours and mine,
Frozen together in a distant time.
I would run mile after mile,
To just see you and that beautiful smile.

17. ANKITA VIBHOR GARG

अंकिता विभोर गर्ग मूल रूप से गंगोह, सहारनपुर की रहने वाली है। ये शिक्षित महिला है। इन्हें पढ़ने, ओर कहानियाँ, शायरी, गजल लिखने का बहुत शौक़ है। ये अपनी लेखनी में अपने दिल की बात लिखती है,इनकी रचनायें सच्चाई बया करती है।ये अपनी 'कलम' के माध्यम से अपनी पहचान बनाना चाहती है। इसके अलावा ये एक सामाजिक कार्यकर्ता भी है। अपना कुछ समय ये सामाजिक सेवा में देती है। नर सेवा नारायण सेवा में ये विश्वास रखती है।आप इनकी रचनाओं को इंस्टाग्राम @ankitavibhorgarg पर पढ़ सकते है।

दर्द

दर्द जब उठता है सीने में,,
कागज पर उतार लेती हूँ
कुछ टूटे ख्वाब सजा लेती हूँ,,
कुछ अश्क़ बहा लेती हूँ,,
बस यूही अपने दर्द को छुपाकर ,,
गम में भी मुस्कुरा लेती हूँ।

अपनी डायरी ओर कलम के साथ,
कुछ वक़्त गुजार लेती हूँ,,
जो नही बया कर सकती बातें,
दर्द भरी सबके सामने ,,
वो दर्द अपनी डायरी मे छुपा देती हूँ।

गम हो या खुशियों के पल,
दोनों में संतुलन बना लेती हूँ,,
कुछ दर्द है तो क्या हुआ ,,
अपनी उमीदों को कभी ,,
हारने नही देती हूँ।

जिंदगी है तो सब कुछ है,,
दर्द आज है तो कल खुशियाँ भी है,,
अपने जनून से हर समस्या का हल
निकाल लेती हूँ,,

कागज ओर कलम है मेरे दोस्त,,
हर दर्द इनके साथ बाँट लेती हूँ,,
विश्वास के दम पर कायम हैं दुनियाँ,,
विश्वास से दर्द को भी हरा देती हूँ।

18. ANKUR MISHRA

बातें अपनी दिल की इस कदर किया करते हैं,
जज़्बात को बयां कोरे पन्ने मे किया करते हैं।

ये है अंकुर मिश्रा जो वर्तमान मे देवास मध्यप्रदेश मे
कार्यरत एक उभरते हुए लेखक हैं जो कि जिंदगी और
नौकरी का संतुलन बनाये रखते हुए अपने लेखन के शौक
को जिंदा रखे हुए हैं। इनकी रचनाये पच्चीस से ज्यादा ई-
बुक/किताबो मे प्रकाशित हो चुकी या होने वाली हैं।
भविष्य मे ये अपनी सभी रचनाओ को खुद की पुस्तक मे
संजोने का ख्वाब रखते हैं। इंस्टाग्राम मे आप इनसे अपने
विचार ankdip2801 मे साझा कर सकते हैं ।

इश्क है तुमसे

अफसाने के फूल बिना खिले थे मुरझाते,
थे बेफ़िक्री के दिन और इत्मिनान की रातें,
यादों की गुल्लक जो भरते चले जाते,
हर किसी से जो चाह के भी कह न पाते,
बड़े अजीब से थे वो दिल्लगी का किस्से,
क्यूँ नही तुम समझे सिर्फ इश्क है तुमसे ।

थे तुम्हारे लिए जीते और सबसे ताने खाते,
चाहकर भी दे न पाये तुमको कई सौगातें,
नासमझ लोग हमे हमेशा ही थे समझाते,
पर तब भी हम तुम्हारी ही राग गुनगुनाते,
बड़े अजीब से थे वो दिल्लगी का किस्से,
क्यूँ नही तुम समझे सिर्फ इश्क है तुमसे ।

कोई नाम भी लेता तुम्हारा तो हम शर्माते,
सभी यार दोस्त भी इसी का फायदा उठाते,
तुमको भाभी कहकर मुझे दिनभर चिढ़ाते,
तुम गुस्सा न हो बस इस बात से थे घबराते,
बड़े अजीब से थे वो दिल्लगी का किस्से,
क्यूँ नही तुम समझे सिर्फ इश्क है तुमसे ।

19. SRAVANI KOMMAYYA

"Believe in what you do.!"

Here Herself Sravani Kommayya who is known as Srk.She believes that writing and exploring are not only hobbies, but also the building blocks of perfect thinking. she is an enthusiastic and pleasant learner and ofcourse a writing passionate. She is in process of becoming her father's pride...

IG - @voice.of_her

LOVE IS!

Love is like a Poem
Which gives you an Enormous Joy
Love is like a Cool breeze
Which helps you for a Fresh Start
Love is like a Mirror
Which reflects your HEART
Love is like a Feeling hub
Which respects each other's Decisions
Love is like a Magic
Which creates the best version of You
Love is like a Life
Which gives you a New Life.!

LOVE IS NOT!

Love is not a Game
To Play with other's Feelings
Love is not a Waste wrapper
To throw after completion of your Work
Love is not a Restriction
To over control your Partner
Love is not Time pass
To only judge their Flaws
Love is not a Knife
To kill someone lively
Love is not a Cage
To seize all their dreams and Desires

Love can kill you
And Love itself can thrill you
So Choose the BEST...

20. PRACHI GUPTA

Prachi Gupta is a Passionate writer who loves to create her imaginary arts in a random canvas. She is pursuing her studies in BBA and lives in Allahabad known as the pure city of Sangam.

She loves to sing and watching movies in her free time.

She is a shy and a open-minded girl at the same time

For more information can follow her and contact:-

Prachiguptt0210@gmail.com

@prachigupta3435

@prachi_gupta_210

NO REGRETS

No regrets for what I did
No doubts of my love
No regrets for what I used to
No doubts how I used
No regrets for what I was believing
No doubts how it came forward
No regrets for my feelings
No doubts of my Heart-breaking
No regrets for the truth
But
I am in just a grief of my parent's trust

21. ANKITA NAHAR

Ankita Nahar, physically she live in AJMER, RAJASTHAN but heartly live in everywhere.

She is too much passionate about writing.

She has always found comfort in words, and that's what attracts everyone. Writing is her therapy, she writes what she feels and experiences in her life. You can take a look at her writings on Instagram @naharankita1

MOMENT

After you left
Every one of life
Spend a lot of time
It was difficult

Especially that
The moment
You I had left
The moment it happened
Like
Death has stopped coming

There was an agony
In my heart after you left
For years to traveler
There is no water in the desert

After you left I knew I was in love
How much is peace
And the pain is so much that it can't be tolerated.

22. NAVEEN BHARDWAJ

Naveen Bhardwaj, a programmer by profession a lover of poetry maker and like reading books and audiobooks and he has telegram channel @TheNBbook

insta I'd na.vin7832

LOVE

Love is the mutual understanding between two it's caring for the other. For some, it is feeling and for others, it is a connection between two hearts. I am not saying loving the right person always works. It can be between family and friends too.
The person you can count on.

Pain can be anything losing someone, the thing you like suddenly out of your sight and you starts worried that's called pain. People feel pain when suffering or it can be in Choosing the wrong part after realizing it's not meant to me. That's a pain for me

Have you ever feel betrayed by your loved ones or a person you count on. Betrayed is sometimes a misunderstanding between two people. You are not confident in your relationship. Or the other person thinking different from you. Or you feel like
Another person ignoring you.

23. SOHINI GHOSH

She's Sohini Ghosh. She's from the city of joy Kolkata. She's 17 years old. She's a writer by passion. She is a motivator and dancer too. She's the founder of writing community words of heart.

HER VOICE OF HEART

Her head is not working till today,
She has no idea why it kills her in this way.

It gets complicated from one thought to another,
She feels like she's no more herself,

She can't cope up with my thoughts
In her head it appears and blast.

She's under so much stress,
She feels to confess,
The pain she have rises up her pressure,
Is there any place which is fine in the hearts
chambers?

Some people say she's so strong,
But in reality they don't know they're saying wrong,
It's a false hope in which she believed for so long.

The beautiful face of mine gives a sweet smile,
But instead the soul says oh girl control it's dying
from a while.

She hates this part of her life,
Which tears her up and increase the pain and to
strive.

She starts her day from a good mood to the spoiled
as hell,
Which whispers in the head she can't tell.

In the whole years most of the days she push herself
through it,
Now a day she remains blank and dont know.

It's going bigger, louder and huge, and strong,
She thinks if she knew what was going on.

She needs to cry,
She wants to cry,
She wants to come out of this and still try.

She wants to weep but she dont know the reason,
She hates this life she dont want it anymore.

Will these feelings last forever?
Will i come out of this biggest fear?
Will there be a day i have no tears?
When will the day come my dear??

She feels like it'll never go,
She feels to fade away and move.

She gets this invisible pain even in her chest,
Her heart says she wants forever rest...

In realistic world it'll never be possible,
That's the first word i got life....

There are no meds that makes me to manage,
The only thing which happened is the damage.

She wants free air,
She wants to move freely without any fears.

Those days she can't hide,
The deepest darkest part she feels inside.

Some days I'm not strong enough,
Some days are too much tough,
When she needed someone to hug her and touch.

But she wores a smile and manage,
She is her only hope and motivates,
She tries to get through it without a single damage.

She wants to go to bed forever...

24. ANJAAN KUMAR DINKAR

When mind capture memories, heart capture happiness and soul capture solace.... Anjan Kumar is a writer and a medical student on his state Uttar Pradesh. He is a science student with PCB who born in a middle class family of age 19, to Arun Kumar Dinkar and Saraswati Devi. He did his high school and intermediate from JNV's. Hobbies are playing, writing, studying etc. If you want to follow him, his instagram id- sars_anjaan_run.

कुछ तो कहना है तुमसे??

कहना तो है सब कुछ तुमसे
पर मैं कुछ कह ना पाता हूं ।
सच तो यह है कि बिन तेरे
अब मैं रह ना पाता हूं।।
क्या चीज हो तुम,मृगनैनी हो।
क्या चीज हो तुम मधुबाला हो ।।
तुम प्यार हो, तुम राग प्रिये।
तुम गीत हो ,तुम हर साज प्रिये।।
मैं एक कहूं ,तुम दो बोलो।
मैं पांच कहूं, तुम दस बोलो।।
अब रह ना पाऊं बिन तेरे
तुम प्यार की हर परिभाषा हो।
तुम चंद्रप्रभा सी दिखती हो
चेहरे का तेज निराला है ।।
तुम कौमुदी सुरबाला सी
यह अंजान तुम्हारा है।
तुम शब्द कहो मैं अर्थ बताऊं
हर पल का में संक्षिप्त बताऊं
हे प्रिय मधुलिका मधुबाला
यह अंदाज हमारा है।।
कहना तो है सब कुछ तुमसे
पर एक कसक सी दिखती हैं
गर खुद से देख मुझे पाती
बेबस इंसान तुम्हारा है।
कहना तो है सब कुछ तुमसे
पर यह हिम्मत से हारा है।।

25. U. Abishek

Abishek.U is an English Literature Graduate, has been working with writing challenged clients for over three years. He loves the way how John Keats pens his Letters. He provides verse writing and article writing based on LGBTQ. His educational background in English Literature and Humanities has given him a broad base to wite on a broad perspective. His writing skills may be confirmed independently on abis_quotes in Instagram.

Bleeding Blue

However I love you, and I did,
I returned again to the plantation.
Home appeared to be so distant,
Caught in the possession of another.
Each dish washed another breath drawn,
The smooth strips against the trees.
My adoration, my miracle, next to me.
Once more, my devils embrace me.
Again did I stop outside of my safe house,
Imploring a noxious, heartless light.
Is it wrong to be so human, my questions,
How is it possible that would dim sky be okay?
Why live if living isn't right,
On the off chance that each whimper ought to be a
cry?
My bed felt more like teeth then, at that point,
Worrying me from each side.
The blossoms sprouted under a night sky,
Enhanced with every one of the things I should've
admitted.
By and by I wind up in that time,
However with you I consider just what I've
subdued.

26. ANKITA SARKAR

Ankita Sarkar is a girl from Jamshedpur. She did her graduation on Hospitality Management and now majoring in Child Psychology. She has published her own book and has been a part of many anthology books. She express her feelings through words.

SENSATIONS

Paint me with your touches,
Paint me with your sensations,
Paint me with your breath,
Paint me with your eyes,
Paint me your smell,
Paint me your care,
paint me with your understanding,
Paint me with your trust,
Last but not least with love.

27. YUVASRI YELLETI

Hello there...She is YuvaSri...a writer by her own Choice...she loves to write and trying to spread her wings through her writings!

A WAKE UP CALL TO SELF-ADMIRATION...

No one is here
To listen to you
To smile with you and
To share your thoughts
So...
Listen to your own words
Smile with your own soul
Share thoughts with yourself
Make this period of darkness
As a period of bright light
That lits up your smile
From inside!

THE CAPTURES...

The best thing about photos is
Even though people leave
Relations dwindle and
The same person can't
Make you smile any more
Photos won't change
The smiles in them won't fade
And the memories they give
Can't be withered!

28. ROZY PAUL

Her name is Rozy Paul. She belongs to the tea-
estate called Dibrugarh, Assam. She has done
M.A.in journalism. Her hobbies are
reading,gardening and cooking. She likes travelling
a lot. Her favourite quote is 'don't harm anyone if
you can't help anyway.'

LOOSELY LOVE

In love trust factor play a vital role. If one can't has that blind faith to someone then it's tougher to get into a relation. But blind faith doesn't mean you carried way after knowing the person's betrayal nature that faith can't come easily in one day that faith has to put by the both persons in gradual manner. When there is lack of trust then there is a scope of parting way or separation actually love is very sensitive relation and every day need effort to make it effortless relation.

29. MANISHA KAMARAJ

She is Manisha Kamaraj pursuing Computer Science Engineering in KSK college of engineering and technology. She currently works at her father's shop as Managing Director. She has capability of writing poem and quotes in both Tamil and English. She has written 30+ anthologies as a Co-author. Follow her at instagram manisha_furniture_mart

I'M IN LOVE WITH YOU!!!

Everyone's love story has,
Some theme or reason,
But in my life,
There is nothing...
His face was unknown,
His bio was unknown,
Only his name is known,
But, something makes me,
In my heart, there is an,
Blooming sound of flowers,
Spreads love fragrance in me...
Finally, there's no reason,
But, I madly love with you...
I don't know, whether you'll be mine,
But I pray, you will be mine,
Oneday, that day was,
More precious day in my lifetime...

30. SAKINA HUSAIN ASGHAR

Sakina Asghar, a young writer started writing at the very tender age of 13. She has been a part of various anthologies of writer's pocket and has been a consistent member of profound writers. In 2020 she received 4th position in National Litreary competition.

People are like sunshine;
They leave you in a time of darkness.

People are like sunshine;
They leave you in a time of darkness.

31. SHWETA SINGH

श्वेता सिंह, ओबरा, सोनभद्र उ.प्र. की रहने वाली हैं। यह एक प्रतिष्ठित शिक्षा संस्थान में सह-समन्वयक / शिक्षक के रूप में शैक्षिक पेशे में है।

इन्होंने 2015 में लिखना शुरू किया था। वह हिंदी में कविताएँ लिखना पसंद करती है और उसे अलग-अलग विधाएँ सीखने का बड़ा शौक है। लेखन इनके लिए एक अराधना जैसे है, जिसमें निरंतरता रखने से मन कभी बोझिल नहीं होता एवं परम आनंद का अनुभव करता है। इन्होंने 50 से भी ज्यादा एंथोलॉजी में सह-लेखक हैं और अपने लेखन कौशल को और चमकाने के रास्ते पर हैं।

मैं तुम्हारा साथ दूंगी

जीवन के हर सफ़र में,
हर ऊँची-निची डगर में,
कदम से कदम मिलाकर,
मैं तुम्हारा साथ दूंगी।
कभी हताशाओं से हार,
जब तुम ठहर जाओगे,
तब उम्मीद बनकर हमेशा,
मैं तुम्हारा साथ दूंगी।
जब कभी तुम रुठ जाओगे,
किसी बात से टूट जाओगे,
उस क्षण भी हमसफर बन,
मैं तुम्हारा साथ दूंगी।
कभी अगर अकेलापन सताएगा,
अपनो का साथ अगर छूट जाएगा,
उस स्थिति में आस बनकर,
मैं तुम्हारा साथ दूंगी।
जब कोई गम तुम्हें सताएगा,
मन को अंधकार ढकता जाएगा,
रौशनी की किरण बन सदैव,
मैं तुम्हारा साथ दूंगी।

32. Samyuktha.S

She is 16 year old aspiring writer and Compiler who started writing in 2018. She loves to write poems, quotes and scribbles. She is interested to learn and explore more about art and different languages.

You came in
Like a sudden shower
But you went away
Just like how you came
Leaving me to beg for
Mending the broken parts
That is left in me
After you shattered
My heart into pieces.

33. NIKITA YADAV

Nikita yadav is an immature writer which is not writer by profession but only loves to write. She belongs to Haryana, Gurgaon City. She is BSC final year medical science student along with this she loves to share her thoughts and experience through her writings. She respect others feelings and emotions an never hurt anyone's feelings and emotions through her content.

She says

"Write the words which comes from depth your heart not for the money"

Never say, "I love you",
If you really don't care...
Never talk about feelings,
If it is not really there...
Never hold my hand,
If you gonna to break my heart...
Never look into my eye,
If you all do is lie...
Never say "Hi",
If you really means goodbye....
If you really means forever
Then say you will try...
Never say forever,
Because forever makes me cry....

34. Dr. SHWETA SINGH

ये एक लेखिका के साथ साथ मोटिवेशनल Youtuber भी है, इनके चैनल का नाम Dr.Shweta Singh है। इनको लिखने का बेहद शौक है। 16 साल से लिख रहे अपनी रचनाएं इनके लेख अखबार और पत्रिकाओं में भी प्रकाशित होते है। इनके लेख आप Blogger, Writco, Dailyhunt, Twitter, Facebook, Instagram, YourQuotes, Website में Dr.Shweta Singh के नाम से पढ़ सकते है। ये पानीपत में रहते हैं।
Insta id:-@dr.Shweta_Singh

My Email is: - Shwetasingh177@yahoo.com

दर्द

वनवास में विरह का दर्द उर्मिला से पूछो, सीता से पूछोगे तो धर्म ही बताएगी!!

मोहब्बत का अर्थ राधा से पूछो,प्यार में बिछड़ने का दर्द क्या होता है वो तो राधा जी ही जाने, रुक्मणि से पूछोगे तो अधिकार ही बताएगी!!

सेवा का मतलब श्रवण कुमार से पूछो, हनुमान जी से पूछोगे तो आनन्द ही बताएंगे!!

जहर का स्वाद शिव से पूछो, मीरा से पूछोगे तो अमृत ही बताएगी!!

और लॉकडाउन का अर्थ गरीबों से पूछो, अमीरों से पूछोगे तो मजा ही बताएंगे!!

प्यार

प्यार में आप यूँ ही सताने लगे,
राह में फूल हम हैं बिछाने लगें।

छोड़ दी है डगर आपने प्रेम की,
रूठ गर हम गए तो मनाने लगे।

बेरुखी ने हमे है सताया बहुत,
बात सारी जहां से छुपाने लगे।

कोशिशें काम ना कर सकी जहाँ,
जाल में फ़ांस कर यूं गिराने लगे।

रौंदकर तुम हमें यार चल ही दिए,
क्रोध में आग बनकर जलाने लगे।

ख्वाब देखे जहां में सभी हैं मिले,
शुक्रिया आपका हम जताने लगे।

आज सीरत न रुसवां यूँ हमें करो,
मोह के मेघ हम को रिझाने लगे।

35. NANDHINEE. S

She is S. Nandhinee doing M.com she has more intrest in writting fantasy stories.

EVERYTHING REMINDS ME OF YOU

Love is not a lust but it's based on loyal and trust worthy relationship forever. The whole story moved beyond two characters Kayal and Kathir. Kayal is a teenage girl. Kayal loves her family members and gives first priority to her family rather than else. Her short term goal is to become a bharathanatyam dancer. She enjoyed each and every moment on her life and lead as she like. She is the princess for her own life. According to her love is a fake relationship and it's all just infactuation about someone. So she doesn't have much involvement in love and she ignores love conversation with her friends. This is how her everyday life goes on.

One day Kayal missed the college bus and planned to go to college by her scooty. At that time there is chill weather and spring season spreads cool breeze everywhere. She felt the pleasant fragrance of beautiful flowers in the garden. She reached college. At that time unexpectedly she met a boy who was good looking, tall and smart was imitated by Kayal. He has smooth hair, moustache, dark eyebrows, six-packs, chubby cheeks, slim fit body. He wore pink shirt and black pant. Kayal was falling in love at first sight at Kathir. Kathir is always be attracted by Kayal like magnetic force attract each other Kathir starts to follow Kayal. He can do anything and everything for Kayal at extend and he express his love towards her unconditionally by proposing her with a red rose. Kayal eyes looks like glittering Sun Rays. It was highly attracted and created some spark in the heart of Kathir. So he can't able to directly face her eyes. Kathir wants to marry Kayal he reveals all his secrets and future plans to her. Even though Kayal loves Kathir she can't able to express her love for her family situations, she hides her love and she accompanies with him and care him like a mother, sister as well as supporting partner. Kathir promised her not to let her down in any critical situation and help her to achieve her ambition as bharatham dancer. Physically, mentally, heartfully, financially Kathir bought the needed things for bharatham to Kayal and he allots best dance master for Kayal to the further practise. Kayal becomes flattered and she enjoyed to wear green saree which had been given by Kathir. There is some twist hide inside that saree, Kathir told Kayal that if she accept his love proposal she should wear that green saree otherwise she wear red saree Kayal got confused. So she wear simple chudi and waiting to see Kathir. Kathir was shocked at presence of Kayal he promise her that eventhough she hasn't declare her love Kathir love for Kayal are always remains constant. Till the end of his lifetime he devoted his mind, heart and soul for the blessings of Kayal. Even at his last breath he utter the name of Kayal and the final face which will always remind him Kayal, Kayal, Kayal. ''Kathir Love for Kayal is a journey, starting at forever and ending at never.'' Thus Kayal stands still in Heart of Kathir at the end of his lifespan. Kayal takes Kathir and his Love as the part of her life so she moved on by smile. Inside of her "Her heart is and always will be only for Kathir''.

36. KAJAL BHARGAV

Kajal bhargav from Lucknow Uttar Pradesh and she's like to writing reading books and Dancing, listening music she's want to become a professor and writer her dream is orphanage homes.

CAREING LOVE...

When you love each other then always remember that 1st things

Loyalty and 2nd Respect.

If you think my attention showing my love then I'll always Am I only attending you.

When I'm sad, you hug me.

When I'm worried, you relax me.

When I'm sick, you take care of me.

It's tough situation to leave someone's.

 When you love them so much.

A true friendship and a true lover never ever over. it's universal facts.

37. RAVISHANKER NISHAD
(ARVI)

यह रविशंकर निषाद है । ये शाखा:- तमनार, जिला:- रायगढ़ (छत्तीसगढ़) के निवासी हैं । इनका जन्म 19 जून 2000 में हुआ था ।। यह अभी इंजीनियरिंग कॉलेज में पढ़ाई कर रहे है । इनकी रुचि कविताएं लिखना है और यह किताबों के शौकीन भी है ।।

राह

गुमसुम सा शांत बैठा मन मेरा
देखती रहती राह तुम्हारी निगाह मेरी ।।
दीपक भी जलता बुझता हताश सा है ।
गलियां घर द्वार वीरान सा है ।।
पायलियां भी मेरी करना चाहती शोर है ।
प्रिय बालम मेरे तू किस ओर है ।।
कंगन की खनखनाहट है
घुंघरू की है झनकार ।।
मेरे दिल की धड़कने बेतहाशा
तुमको रही है पुकार ।।
घर आ जाओ प्रियतम मेरे
शाम ढल गई है ।।
देखत राह तुम्हारी मेरी
अखियां थक गई है ।।

38. MEENAKSHI

Meenakshi, she is from Punjab. Being an introvert, she loves writing her thoughts and observations in the form of quotes, poems and stories.

1. कह दूँ या चुप रहूँ।
या करू लिख के ब्यान, मैं ख्याल अपने।।
एहसास-ए-दिल मेरा, अंजाम से डरता है।
जिगरी यार ना छूट जाए, जुल्म-ए-मोहब्बत में।।

2. ताउम्र इस फ़िराक़ में निकाल दी
कहीं वों हमसे युदा न हो जाए
जब वक़्त आया युदाई का
तो मालूम हुआ, हम कभी साथ थे ही नहीं

3. वो शोक के लिए प्यार करते थे
और हमें शोक प्यार करने का था
शोक उनका भी बदला, हमारा भी
उन्हें किसी ओर से प्यार हो गया
हमे प्यार से नफरत

39. DEESHA SONI

Deesha Soni...a Post Graduate and M.phil adorns the hat of a multitasker of an educationist, artist, poet, photographer, author, blogger, homemaker, wife and mother... She has 10 years experience in the field of Education as a Professor and Coordinator.Deesha has various publications to her credit in national and international levels. Deesha has various published works to her credit... she has two books published on Amazon... named 'Just thoughts' and 'Random thoughts on pandemic'. Kindle edition and more than 100 plus published works on various online platforms of... Deesha has been twice nominated for Author of a week award by Storymirror and has also won various recognitions in penning stories and write-ups.. At National and International levels... Deesha has various published works to her credit... she has two books published on Amazon... named 'Just thoughts' and 'Random thoughts on pandemic'.Kindle edition has also won many prizes in National and international levels in many write-ups... Deesha has also published her works in 300 plus anthologies of multiple genres.

THAT I HAVE ABSOLUTELY NO HOPE.....

I'm broken and have lost the hope...
I'm dead...and my body is hanging from a rope...
Tears have dried...
An Ocean I've cried...

You used me for advantage which gave me a bad
stroke....
You ditched me... I'm ripped apart...my heart
crushed and broke...
I was stabbed at the back...
Deep within I have wounds and crack...

Though for I future I had high hope...
My mother warned me.... with you I shouldn't
elope....
I had dreams with you to see the globe...
But I was dejected and you said nope...

I'm taken on four shoulders...in white shroud I'm
enloped...
But in my lifeless eyes...the memories of your
violence and threat still grope...
Your love for me was rhe only positive hope...
But my trust you broke... pushed and threw it from
a slope....

You were so hopeless...
That I have absolutely no hope...
That I have absolutely no hope...

40. YOGESH GURJAR CHINU

इनका नाम योगेश गुर्जर है और निकनेम चीनू है, यह उत्तरप्रदेश के गौतम बुद्ध नगर जिले से है। इन्हें थॉट्स लिखना और पढ़ना बहुत पसंद है, पोएट्री और कोट्स 1300 से ज्यादा लिख चुकी है। 450 Anthology में Co-author के रूप में लिख चुकी है। इनकी पहली सोलो बुक जिसका नाम (सच्ची बातें "चीनू") है।

इंतजार

दिन हो या रात याद तेरी ही,
दिल बेचैन अब अच्छा लगता है,

अब हर पल तुम्हारा इंतज़ार में,
दरवाजे को ताकतें रहना भी अच्छा लगता है,

खड़े रहना दहलीज़ पर,
पलकें झुकाए अच्छा लगता है,

तू आये ना आये बस यूहीं तेरा,
बेवजह इंतज़ार करना अब अच्छा लगता है,

झूठा ही सही अपने ही दिल को,
झूठा दिलासा देना अब अच्छा लगता है,

तेरे सिवा अब कोई नहीं मन को लुभाता है,
एक तू ही है जो दिल को भाता है,

तेरे इंतजार में सब कुछ भूल जाना अच्छा लगता है,
बस तेरे प्यार में ही रहना अच्छा लगता है....!!

व्याकुल मन

व्याकुल मन स्थिर ना हो,
तड़प तड़प वो जाये,

ना जाने कब किस ओर,
पंछी बन उड़ जाये,

प्रेमी बन प्रेम में,
प्रीत प्रीत चिल्लाये,

विष का प्याला यूं पीयें,
जैसे कोई प्यास बुझायें,

उलझन मन में यूं बस जाये,
बस उम्मीद ही साथ निभाये,

कंटक पथ पर यूं चल जाये,
जैसे कोई सेज पर चल जाये,

फूल बन कर यूं खिल जाये,
जैसे कोई सुगंध मन को भा जाये....!!

41. SHIVANG SHARMA

शिवांग शर्मा आज के युग के नए शायर हैं। शायर साहब वाराणसी के निकट स्थित मऊ जिले से आते हैं। इन्होंने कई पुस्तकों में सह - लेखक और संकलक के रूप में काम किया हैं। शायर साहब वर्तमान समय में राष्ट्रीय प्रौद्योगिकी संस्थान पटना से इंजीनियरिंग कर रहे हैं। इनके लिखने का सिलसिला क्यूँ शुरू हुआ ये आपको नीचे के लेख में दिखेगा - " मिलता नहीं मुझे कोई अकेला रहता हूँ मैं , लेता हूँ सहारा कलम का पन्नों पे चीख देता हूँ मैं। " Insta I'd - @__dil_e_alfaaz__

कमज़ोर होता जा रहा हूँ...

बड़ा ही कमज़ोर होता जा रहा हूँ
अपनों से हारता जा रहा हूँ,

न जाने ऐसा क्यों हैं
ग़मों में मुस्कराते जा रहा हूँ,

जाने किस ज़माने से मैं
अपनी तकलीफें छुपाते जा रहा हूँ,

पहने रहता हूँ झूठी हसी
चेहरे को मुखौटों में छुपाते जा रहा हूँ,

मुश्किल हो रही है जीने में
आहिस्ता-आहिस्ता मारता जा रहा हूँ,

वफादार रहने की जिद में
खुशियों को त्यागते जा रहा हूँ,

बड़ा ही कमज़ोर होता जा रहा हूँ
अपनों से हारता जा रहा हूँ।

42. BHARGAVI. V

Bhargavi. V M.A English literature. Nandha arts and science college Erode Tamilnadu. Writer, Translator, compiler and public speaker. Head of Om Yodha Writer's club. Founder of Yodha Group of Entrepreneurs.

INKED DREAMS....

Raging dreams in
Rowing streams
Rivalling spirits of
Rude hostiles..
Routed inside the
Rooted memories..
Rifled shots of
Ransacking life breaks..
Ridiculous riddles of
Rumbling wind...
Real measures of
Reel world...
Remembering the ride
Reaping my ego
Ripped in hell...
Rating the riverflow
Life goes on like
How the stars glow.

43. CATHERINE SHEENA

Sheena Catherine is a girl with plenty of dreams. She likes to write poems, short stories, quotes etc. She is a broad minded person. She believes that words speak greater than action so she writes from her heart.

MY DESTINY

When I woke up from my sleep,
My pillow was wet from my tears.
I cried all night,
For someone to show up in my Life,
To make my life merrier.
Days gone, by gone.
No one showed up yet.
I'm still waking up with wet eyelids.
Why the life that's supposed to be mine doesn't fit to
me?
Why I'm different from others?
Why can't I be loved like others?
Where it started to go wrong?
I don't know.
But somewhere deep inside my heart,
I still believe,
You'll come for me, My Destiny.

44. SRIJA SADHUKHAN

Srija Sadhukhan is 19 years old girl studying BSc Biotechnology. Love to write poetry and a book worm too.

FEELINGS

In the depth of despair and loneliness
He held my hand
To set a journey full of high tides
With a seagulls flying overhead.
Eyes whisper with tranquilizing waves
Where my soul travels with you.

I am drowning in an ocean of love
Love hit me like the ocean hits the seashore
My heart beats with unwanted rhythm
Seashells lying on the seabed.
 Deeper than our feelings
Your love for me was never suspense.

45. NIKHIL JAIN

निखिल जैन, एक नवयुग के लेखक हैं, जो की धुले, महाराष्ट्र से संबंध रखते है। ये अपना ज्ञान दूसरो के साथ साझा करना, यात्रा करना, नई नई खोज करना और रचनात्मकता का बेहद शौक रखते है। इन्हें लिखना पसंद है, और इनका मानना है, कि लेखन से हम अपनी आंतरिक भावनाओं का भली भांति बखान कर सकते है। ये 20 से अधिक पुस्तकों के संकलनकर्ता रह चुके है और इनका स्वयं का एक ऑनलाइन प्रकाशन "unite publication" भी है। इनसे जुड़ने के लिए आप संपर्क कर सकते हैं इंस्टाग्राम : @love.vibes143 ईमेल - love.vibes143@outlook.com

मुझे उनसे प्यार जो हो गया था...

जब ये नैना जब टकराए थे उनसे,
दिल बेक़रार सा हो गया था,
शायद मुझे उनसे प्यार हो गया था...

नजरें झुका कर चली आती थी वो मेरे सामने,
आँखों ही आँखों से बातें हो जाया करती थी,
शायद मुझे उनसे प्यार हो गया था...

जबसे लगा बैठा था ये दिल उनसे,
दिन बेचैन रातें हसीन, सब कुछ बदल गया था,
शायद मुझे उनसे प्यार होगया था...

मेरी हर दुआ हर इबादत में शामिल थी वो,
हर मन्नत में खुदा से उसको मांगा करता था,
शायद मुझे उनसे प्यार जो हो गया था...

जब एक दिन बयां की उसने अपने दिल की बात,
किसी और को चाहती हूं में,खोला ये राज़,
देख उसके आंखों में झलकती खुशी,
ना कर सका में अपने प्यार का इजहार,
शायद इसी को कहते है सच्चा प्यार,
क्यूंकि मुझे उनसे प्यार जो हो गया था...

46. SONIYA VARGHESE

Soniya Varghese is a writer filled with her own euphoria. She is a person who remains euphoric to see the kindred and emotions evoked around her. She is an author who handles mostly romantic themes and fun thrillers which is both for teens and adults. Especially anyone who have once fallen in love in their life. Whenever she writes she takes a part from her own life. Her writings reflects all that she had experienced in her life. Anyone who reads all her writings can connect it with her life. Instagram: soniya__ varghese, Facebook: Soniya Varghese, Twitter: @SoniyaVarghese8

EVERY EMOTIONS I FOUND IN HIM

He was the only one who could tame me. He was the first love of my life. I never knew what it felt to be loved but after meeting him I knew the meaning of true love. He always cared me like a baby. I loved him so much that I could barely remember a day without him after we have met. Love was a special sort of emotion which gives us a reason to live.

Loving is another thing. After knowing what is love we start to love anyone. He at first taught me what love was. After Knowing what was love I started to love him. Loving him was realisation that there can be no one else in this whole world whom I could love like I love him.Loving him brought every sort of happiness to my life. And loving hime became a reson for my existence.

Loved. Being lived is a blessing. Being loved by the person whom we love is a special feeling. It confirms or assures that we are safe with them. Being loved is to be cared and to be taken care of. So He was the only one made me realise all these 3 emotions. He taught me the meaning of love, then i started loving him. And being loved by him was a bonus. He was that treasure box where i found all the emotions I wanted to sustain.

47. AKKSHAYA PRASANNA

She is Akkshaya Prasanna. I know her since 17 years. She completed B.A in hindi at the early age of 12. Also adding one more feather to a crown. She completed diploma in Sanskrit. She learned carnatic music and bharathanatyam. Now she is incarnated as a writer. Started to travel with words and explore knowledge. Adding a golden line to her crown again.

NO LOVE

Everything is lovely Until
It happens hastly
He came around
And asked
To walk along
On the ground
I say......
Let me Have
Some time
Then...
I want him
As mine
DAYS ... Went with him
He left me in rim
I know being loved is stupendous
Staying in love is arduos.

48. AKSHAYA MURUGESAN

Writer called Akshaya Murugesan. She is studying English literature. Her passion isn't writing. Has she had interest to write poems. Just, she wants to give voice to her thoughts. So, she chooses to write poems. Her Colourful dreams and thoughts being as a text format in her works. She was worked in 40+ Anthologies as a Co-author and she is also a Compiler too. She is Selenophile. She tries to give her best in whatever she was in. Her thoughts were common and her words were realistic.

LOVE FOR MY LOVE.....!

Oh....My dear Love....!
Veracity is always ultimate,
I wish you to be with me;
I'd a dream....,
Which made my day awfy.

Best Bonding never ended up,
Bonding between us is unpredictable;
As I got you, you got me
And we find happiness in us....!

If any questioned
What is Love.....?
I will show them our Relationship
As an answer....!

Yes....! Love does wonders,
I realised by My Love;
No more queries,
I love you the most......!

49. PAYAL KAMADI

Payal Kamdi from Maharashtra. A girl with passion in writing mess with her heart and mind.The picking of ink and fell down of paper which cames along shadow. She is penning her thoughts by penname Nityashree. She believes writing helps to concrete thoughts and manifest faster. Being a self lover she is binder of relationships too. Love can loose you but gives you hope of finding stars she convinced.

The sky is different for everyone
You may see light other can see dark
But what's the best you see you own perspective.

In the constant cycle of love have you left love
If you answered yes then it's ok
If you answer no then love doesn't arrived.

50. ANAMIKA

Anamika is an art preceptor by profession and belongs to Brass city Moradabad, Uttar Pradesh. She loves to articulate her thoughts and views in a poetic manner. It gives her peace and satisfaction. According to Anamika love is pure form and can be linked up with anyone. She is a good observer who imbibes her thoughts by observing nature around her. She has participated in 80+ anthologies before this.So, here are some of the thoughts and views expressed by Anamika, hope you all will like it….. To read from Anamika's pen follow her on Insta@Anamika.Writes

SEARCH OF A SOUL

Every soul search love,
Every soul desires to be loved,
Love can bind souls,
Love can shatter souls,
Only a person shattered from inner soul ,
Can value those,
Feelings of a bumble - bee towards flower,
Is real love rare???
No one knows how to shower,
Looking for an innocent smile,
Even on unknown faces is love & delight,
Being broken and still protecting others to be
broken is love....
Broken souls know the pain and
Don't want to continue the chain,
They just spread only love
As love messengers are like dove....

51. VAISHNAWI KUMARI

वैष्णवी कुमारी विभिन्न प्रकाशनों के साथ 100+ सफल रचनाओं के साथ-साथ 10+ विश्व रिकॉर्ड एंथोलॉजी के सह-लेखक हैं। उनकी पुस्तकों को कई प्रसिद्ध प्रकाशनों से प्रशंसा और मान्यता मिली है। यह खूबसूरत कवयित्री पटना, बिहार से ताल्लुक रखती है, और वह एनएसआईटी, बिहटा, पटना से एक आगामी कंप्यूटर विज्ञान स्नातक है। अपने पिता से प्रेरित होने के बाद, उन्होंने लेखन के साथ-साथ नृत्य और गायन के अपने जुनून को तेज कर दिया है।एक लेखक के रूप में 4 आगामी परियोजनाएं हैं। उनका मानना है कि कविता दुनिया को बदल सकती है, और वह इसका इस्तेमाल युवाओं को प्रेरित करने और सशक्त बनाने के लिए करती है। आप व्यक्तिगत रूप से उनके इंस्टाग्राम हैंडल @kumarivaishnawi से संपर्क कर सकते हैं और उनकी अद्भुत रचनाओं को देखने के लिए @mystic.vaishu को फॉलो कर सकते हैं।

किस्मत

लगता है हमारी किश्मत हमसे रूठ गई है,
सारी ख्वाहिशें मर रहीं हैं,
करते थे हम जिनसे मोहब्बत बेपनाह
आज उन्हें अच्छे से देखने को निगाहें तरस रहीं हैं।।।
कमी महसूस होती होगी उन 4 दिवारो में हमारी,
रातों को शायद सोने ना दे पायल की छन-छन आहट
हमारी,
बस कुछ ऐसा ही सफ़र था अपना
खत्म हो गया रिश्तों की कारवां हमारी।।।
बड़ी शिद्दत से अपनी किताब में हमारे पते को छिपाकर
रखा है उन्होंने,
और हमने देख क्या लिया वो तो हमें जासूस समझ
गए।।।।

52. PRAGATI GIRI

Pragati Giri bought from UP state district Varanasi.She has graduated in BSc from biology stream.She loves nature and loved to help people's who comes in seekness.In writing industry she is a writer, Co-author, Compiler & project head in three Publications. IG: @writerpragati5409, @@__pragati_giri3 Blogger: pragatigiriwrites.blogsot.com/

PERFECT PEACE

Love can be invisible but it won't be change if it comes from pure heart.

Like season we can't deny when it comes at any time as well as love for another person who is closed with you, then you can't deny to them like any whether.

53. Dr. SEEMA DANSANA

वह एक AYUSH DOCTOR है। उन्होंने S. S. N. Ayurved college & RI, Nrusinghnath से B.A.M.S की पढ़ाई पूरी की है। उनकी ताकत आत्म-प्रेरित, मेहनती और एक अनुशासित व्यक्ति हैं। उनकी अल्पकालिक लक्ष्य हर छोटे सपने को पूरा करना है और उनकी दीर्घकालिक लक्ष्य एक अच्छी स्थिति हासिल करना है जहां वह अपना करियर बना सकते है और गरीब लोगों की मदद कर सकते है।

वह बहुत अच्छी डॉक्टर है, वह मरीज की बात को अच्छी तरह से समझती है और उनकी देखभाल ठीक से करती है , वह लिखना भी पसंद करती है। उसने आज तक 100+ एंथोलॉजी में भाग लिया है। वे अपने लेखन को बेहतर बनाने के लिए दैनिक प्रतियोगिता में भाग लेते हैं।

उन्हे Instagram- @ mydairy144 पर follow करें ,Email- seemadns571@gmail.com,YourQuote ऐप पर मेरे विचारों का पालन करें https://www.yourquote.in/my_dairy

मैं इश्क लिखूं या उसे लिखूं

मैं इश्क लिखूं या उसे लिखूं
क्या फर्क है इन दो शब्दों में
मैं छत पर हूं, वो आंगन में
उसे देख कर मैं क्या गजब लिखूं

उसे देखकर हम तो बेवस हैं
क्या अपनी बेबसी को कत्ल लिखूं
मैं रास्ता हूं, वो मंजिल है
किस शक्ल में खुद को सफल लिखूं

गली से मेरी गुजरे वो,
महक उठे हैं सब चौराहे
इन गलियों का कायल में,
गलियों को ताजमहल लिखूं

वह बादल है, जाने कब बरसे
एक बूंद भी उसकी पा लूं तो,
मैं उस दिन खुद को दरिया लिखू......!!!!

54. Jasmine Panda

जास्मिन पंडा एक सुआलोचिका, सुउपस्थापिका और सुलेखिका है जो साहित्य में विशेष रुचि रखती हैं। वह राज्यपाल पुरस्कार प्राप्त व रसायन विज्ञान में स्वर्ण पदक प्राप्त यूनिवर्सिटी टॉपर हैं। एक विज्ञान की छात्रा होने के साथ ही वह एक कला प्रेमी मेहनती लड़की है, जो चित्रांकन में रुचि रखने वाली एक आल राउंडर पुरस्कार प्राप्त भी है। जास्मिन ईश्वर पर अतुट विश्वास रखती हैं। प्रकाशित पुस्तकें - अलंकृता, बिंदी, साज़-ई-हस्ती, ख्वाब, यूफोरिया, द ट्रावेल ट्रवेस्ट्री, सीजन्स, अफशियनाडो, रंग, स्टरियोटाइप्स, पोएटेस्टर, जर्नी २०२०, राईटर बड्स, भॊ अफ़ प्रोटेक्शन भाग-२, यादें बचपन की, अनकही बातें, तजुर्बा ए-ज़िन्दगी, पोएम पिल, पिंजरा, मेरा भारत महान, माइंड और हार्ट, अंदरमहल, सोशियल इश्यूज़, परमिला, सिब्लिंग्स, वी सैड ऐस, पिता से है नाम मेरा, अंब्रियोसाल, आम् आई द वन हू लॉस्ट, एलरमेंट, ट्रानकृती, क्यूरियोसिटी, स्पीकिंग मई तृत, तेरा शहर...

क्या यही सच्चा प्यार था!

खुद को भुलाकर तुझमें जी रही थी,
नींदों को गवांकर सपने देख रही थी,
तेरा हात थामकर आसमान में उड़ रही थी,
खुद से अलग होकर मै प्यार कर रही थी!!
क्या यही सच्चा प्यार था?

वर्तमान तो मेरा सिर्फ तू ही था,
भविष्य के बारे में तो सोचा भी न था!
दुनिया भुलाकर सिर्फ तू ही मेरी दुनिया था,
बस, और कोई नहीं सिर्फ तू ही तू था!
क्या यही सच्चा प्यार था?

इतनी सिद्दत से मेरा तुझको चाहना,
रात - दिन बस तू ही तू करना,
तेरे लिए जीना, तेरे लिए मरना,
कोशिश थी बस तेरे ही दिल में रहना!
क्या यही सच्चा प्यार था?

मेरे सपने भूलकर तेरे सपनों में जीना,
तेरे सुख-दुख का साथी बन जाना,
अपनों को छोड़कर तुझे अपना बनाना,
तू जैसा चाहे जब चाहे वैसे ही करना!
क्या यही सच्चा प्यार था ?

इन आंखों में तुने कितने सपने दिए,

छोड़ आई थी मैं घर-बार तेरे लिए,
क्या ग़लत था उस दिन का निर्णय मेरा,
बहुत अच्छा लगा वो उपहार तेरा,
तब समझ गई मैं, हां यही सच्चा प्यार था मेरा!
तब समझ गई मैं, हां यही सच्चा प्यार था मेरा!

मां बाप को भुलाकर जो तेरे पीछे भाग रही थी,
अपने कैरियर के बदले जो तुझपे मर रही थी,
बता दिया तुने मुझे सच्चा प्यार क्या होता है?
अब पूछना नहीं पड़ता, मेरी सफलता बता देती है!!!
सच्चा प्यार यही होता है....
सच्चा प्यार यही होता है.....

LOVE
LOVING
LOVED